Different Variety

BETTIE ROBERSON

ISBN: 9781490774565 (sc)
ISBN: 9781490774572 (e)

Trafford rev.   06/16/2016

www.trafford.com
North America & international
toll-free: 1 888 232 4444 (USA & Canada)
fax: 812 355 4082

CONTENTS

ACKNOWLEDGMENTS

First and formost, I give thanks to the most High God, who is the author and finisher of my faith, for He is my life, and without Him, I can't do nothing. He is our all and all. He will protect you, provide, heal and deliver.

To my daughter Felicia her husband, and the grand childrens Ja Quan, Ja Quill, and Jayman. I love you so much. Thanks to my neice Tammy, for been a helper, to get this book accomplish. To all my other family members thank you, from my heart to your heart. To my chosen prayers members, thanks for allowing me to be a part of you. We give God all the glory, for He is worthy to be praise.

The mission statements is.

The joy of the Lord is our strengthen with God all things are possible, and to let others know, to hold on to God's unchanging hands

Bettie Roberson

I accepted Jesus Christ in my life at the age of 11, not alway doing things write. But forever standing in the gab for, His forgiveness

I have one daughter and 3 grandchildren. Whom I love dearly. Worked on one job for many years. Now that I have retired, I just love it.

I enjoy day trips, going to church, and riding around the different cities and playing on my Ipad.

Again, I thank God for this opportunity, for giving me, the go power to write the book. Call Different Varieties. It will be based of diffence topic. I have been loving to write, for a long time. Now though the Trafford Publishing Company, God has giving me the opportunity once again to do so, In such a time as this

Pray that in reading the book, that everyone enjoys it, and someone be touch with God's love. My favor scripture, in found in John 3:16 it reads as thus.

John 3:15. N.I.V

Bettie Roberson

For God so loved the world that he gave his one and only son, that whoever believes in him shall not perish, but have eternal life.

This is one of my favor scriptures, for God, does not want any one to perish; He gave of His one and only son. So that we can have life, and have it more abundantly.

For His love endures forever.

(The End)

PART 1

Encouraging Words

As people in this generation we need encouragements, follow by hope, we can hope on many things, such as a job, car, homes carreer, but this can be wrongly taken with out. Others, giving us encouragedment. The book of Exodus 18:1-9, spcaks about how Moses had a family re union, though his father-in-law Jethro, had to bring Moses, wife and children to him, he still needed to be encourage. Moses was a leader, yet, he needed encouragement. All people needs to be encouraged, it does not matter about their position, the word is to encouraged. Moses bowed down before his father in-law, out of love and respect.

He humble himself before Jethro, Moses. Also shared all the maraculous interventions, that God, had done for him.

Jethro was so supportive to Moses and he encouraged Moses to do the Lords will

Moses was taking to many responibilities upon himself, therefore Jethro, his father-in-law, became concern.

He counseled Moses to appoint good to take over, so that Moses himself, would not be so overwhelmed, with the leadership position.

Moses listen to Jethro and incorported a system that was balanced for the community as well as for his family

Moses, was encourage, because before his father-in law spoke to him. He was listen to the people of Isreal, both night and day; trying to solve their problems.

Encouragement is an act of kindness, to encourage someone
It has to be geniene.

Be compassinate, never take matter's upon ourselves

If a time set, to encourge others, simple things as a smile, hello,
thank you, and say something (nice) about the person.

Its so important to encourage others, also encourged your self as
well. Paul encourge himself to be content.
David encourage himself by dancing before the Lord.

Joshua 1:9.

Have not I commanded thee, be strong and of good courage, be
not afraid, neiether be thou dismayed, for the Lord thy God is
with thee whither-so-ever thou goest.

2 Timothy 1:7

For God has not gives us the spirit of fear, but of power and of
love and of a sound minds

Phillipain's 4:13

I can do all things though Christ which strengthen me.

As we go out on our daily routines, remember to encourage
someone.

To be one is to reach one.

Jeremiah 29:11

Not forsaking the thoughts that I think towards your saith the Lord, thoughts of peace, and not evil to give you an expected end.

<u>In my conclusion</u>: The more people we encouraged, will be multipied back Amen!

PART 2

A Letter To Jesus

Dear God

I thank you for this day. As I am writing to you today. 7-12 13, this day is my husband birthday. Happy birthday to a wonderful man. RIP. I love you.

Lord, all the glory and the honour belongs to you. You have brought us though this and that. Thank you, for your tender mercy. Thank you, for providing for us as we go though our own trails and turbulation, thank you for a break though.

You are the all knowing and mighty God, whom we trust adore and worship. You has blessed us in many ways

Our hearts sometimes are broken, but you are the mender of a broken heart., A lot of times, as people, we do not keep our promise, yet you still forgive us, and always love us. Dear Lord again our tongue needs to be tanged, help us to tang our tongue. Keep it from been the root of evilness. Help us to speak peace in others lives. This letter is for so many people that are hurting and need you as their personal savior, if prehaps they dont know the way. Let the people read this scripture

Romans 10:9-10

(9) That if thou shalt confess with thy mouth the Lord Jesus, and shalt believe in thine heart that God hath raised him from the dead, thou shalt be saved.

(10) For with the heart man believeth unto righteousness, and with mouth confession is made is made unto salvation.

(11) For the scripture saith whosoever believeth on him shall not be ashamed.

We love you so much Lord therefore this letter will always be open from our heart to yours.

Thank you, again for all the wonderful blessing that you grant all of us that crys out to you.

Love Ya!

PART 3

Poems

Life Lived Poems.

Life is living
And total living
It will push us over
Kick us while we are down
And hit us as we rise
Everything will not be against us
Things will also change us
But we get to choose the one that will help us.
Listen to your heart
Follow your dreams. Let it go
Allow no one to tell you your capabity.
Push for the limits
Bend the rules
And enjoy life
Laugh as much as possible
Live as long as you can.
Love all
Trust God
Believe in yourself
Never lose faith in God
Settle for nothing: do your best
Take risks
Live life to the fullest
Life is a gift
Appreciate all the blessing
Jump on all the opportunities
Love everyone regardless
Never forget where you came from

Remember to move forward
Fine your purpose in life
And live thought it
Never waver, always abide in our savior, the Lord Jesus Christ
Live, live, live, and hold your head up.
Never look down, unless you are tieing your shoe or someone else
Life is worth the challenge. (Hallala).

Bettie Roberson

<u>What if</u>!

What if I can (fly) will you make me a bird.

What if I could (sing) would you give me a plane

What if I had, all the money that I could spend.

But no (love) was found deep with in.

It will mean nothing because (love) covers all.

    To God be the glory.

(<u>Rest</u>)

Rest in peace, my love one
Rest in peace
Sleep on my loved one sleep on.
Your pain is gone
Your cry is over
Eternally, essentially at rest
Part me, part you, part child, by angels blessed.

Thank you for the lovely card heartfelt, welcome and warm kind words and friends with calm

For lost is always hard opening to sympathy that comes from the heart.
Rest on our loved one, rest on. Time will mend our broken heart. Rest on.

The End.

PART 4

Bible Scripture

Psalms 23. K.J.V

A Psalm of David

(1) The Lord is my shephard, I shall not want.

(2) He maketh me to lie down in green pastures, He leadeth me beside the still waters.

(3) He retoreth my soul, he leadeth me in the path of righteouness for his name sake

(4) Yea, though I walk through the valley of the shadow of death, I will fear no evil; for thou art with me, thy rod and thy staff they comfort me.

(5) Thou preparest a table before me in the presence of mine enemies. Thou anointest my head with oil. My cup runneth over.

(6) Surely goodness and mercy shall follow me all the days of my life, and I will dwell in the house of the Lord forever.

PART 5

Remember /vs /We Know

Remember, the good old days, when we could, walk and feel the sunshine.

We could walk in the rain, at the end of the raindrops, their was a rainbow, that had multitude of color.

But, do remember the rainbow, was a promise from God, that the earth would never have a over flow of water.

No Matter What!

PART 6

Prayers For All Occasions

There are so many things to pray about. First and for most pray for <u>self</u>.

This is not naming all the prayers, but pay attention to the following.

Pray for familys, pray for leadership. Pray for the sick, pray for peace pray for the bereveaments, pray for Ireal, pray for help, pray for salvation, pray for repentance, pray for healing, pray for wisdom, pray for spiritual growth, pray for marry couples, pray for childres, pray for prayers, pray for strenth, pray for knowledge.

This list, again goes, on, on, and on; the key words, are to pray with an sincere heart.

To God Be the Glory!

PART 7

Let it go, Just Do it

Let go self. Ask God for help.

Let go greed, God will supply your need.

Let go doubt, God will bring you out.

Let go fear, God wipes away, every tear.

Enjoy life everyday, and don't forget to pray.

Dont waste a moment in life.

Time will come, when everything will be alright

Let it go! And just do it.

PART 8

Be Thankful

Be thankful, for all you have.

Be thankful, for the sun.
Be thankful for the rain.

Be thankful for everything
Be thankful for the smallist thing.

Take time to laugh!
Take time to smile
Take time to cry.
Take a break.
Give back
Love more
And just say thank you!

For the care's of this life is only passing though

Learn to say, thank you!

PART 9

Seige The Moment

Dont give up.
In every opportunity
Seige it.

Dreams will come
Vision's will come
Step out on faith
Believe it!
Recieve it!
Achieve it!

Dont walk away.
Dont sit down, or sleep.

Search high
Go above and beyond.

Reach for the sky
Look for goodness
Look for greatness
Look for the better
And you will be the best.

PART 10

Different Songs

1st Song Even Me!

Even me Lord
Even me
Even me Lord
Even me.

I sing this song
Even me
I pray this prayer
Even me

I bow my head
Even me
I bow my head
Even me

I thank you Lord
Even me
I thank you Lord
Even me.

I love you Lord
Even me
I love you Lord
Even me.

I give you praise
Even me
I give you praise
Even me

Even me Lord, even me;
Even me Lord, even me.

Jesus!

Jesus in the morning.
Jesus at noon day
Jesus in the evening
Jesus at night.

I say, Jesus, Jesus, Jesus.

Jesus in the morning
Jesus in the noon day
Jesus in the evening
Jesus at night

He will fight your battle
He will answer prayer
Call upon His name
He will be just there

I say, Jesus, Jesus, Jesus.

He, has all power
He, owns everything

Jesus, Is His Name

Black Birds

Black birds do sing
Black birds do sing
Black birds do sing
And they make noise, for the Lord.

Black birds do fly
Black birds do fly
Black birds do fly
Making noise, for the Lord

They gather in one place.
They gather in one place
They gather in one place
Making noise for the Lord

Black birds sing
Black birds fly
Black birds gather

Up lifting the name of the Lord.

(Journey)

On this life journey
You praise the Lord

On this life journey
You praise the Lord.

On this life journey
You praise the Lord

On this life journey
You bless His name

On this life journey
You bless His name

On this life journey
You give Him thanks!

On this life journey
You give Him thanks!

He will make a way
Out of no way

So keep the faith!
And always pray.

For this journey
Will end someday

The Bucket List

Life is like a river
That has its ups and down's

But when you seek Him
All love is found.

Whats on your bucket list to accomplish.
Just to name a few.

(1).   Read 15 books
(2).   Write a book
(3).   Fly a kite
(4).   Ride a bike
(5).   Go on vacation
(6).   Go to the zoo
(7).   Overcome fear
(8).   Climb a tree
(9).   Just let it be
(10). Be kind to others
(11) Love every body
(12) Go back to school.
(13). Follow the rules
(14). Go to the park
(15). Eat watermelon in the dark
(16). Be on T.V.
(17). Lead someone to Christ
(18). Be a mentol.
(19). Write your own play
(20). Learn to pray
(21). Go to the beach

22. Stay home mom
23. Go to the prom
(24) Just say no
(25) Just say yes. Do you best

All things on this bucket list can be accomplish.
    If we only stay focus.

The Blind Man!

Blind man says, Money money, money
Disciples, says, Did his parents sin.
Jesus, says, No, he was born blind
Narrator, So Jesus spat on the ground, and made mud, then put it on the man's eyes
Jesus, Go wash your eyes in the pool of Siloam.
Blind man, Praise God, I can see, I can see.
Neigbors, Isn't this guy who was blind and begging for money
Townsfolfs, No, it just looks like him
Blind man, Yes, it is me, I can see, I can see!
Townsfolfs, Where is this man named Jesus.
Blind man, How should I know,? I went to wash my eyes like, he told me to
Jesus, Do you believe in the Messiah,
Blind man, Who is he that I can believe
Jesus, You are looking at him, it is me
The Blind man was blind, but now he can see.

The Story of the Lost Son

Then he said, there once was a man that had two sons. The younger said to his father, I want whats coming to me right now!. So the younger son, took his portion, and went to a far country. While there, he wasted all the money he own.

Then comes a famine, in the land. The younger son, began to hurt, living among the pigs, he had no food, no shelter, no family, then one day, as he way lying with the pigs. He came to himself, and said, I will go back home to my father. I will say to him, father I have sinned against God. I dont deserve, to be called your son. It say, the father saw, his son a distant off. He ran to his son, embrace him, kiss him, gave him, the best of food and said to him, Welcome home, your sins are forgiven. Amen!

And David said to Saul, Let no mans heart fail because of him, thy servant will go and fight with this Philistine. 1 Samuel 17:32

All of us face giants, from time to time. These gaints try to do some things to us that Goliath did to the Army of Isreal, - intimidate and bring fear. When the giants come we have to make a choice, are we going to let them make us afraid or stand up to them through the power of the Lord. David made the chose to not look at the size of the giant, but at the size of His God, so instead of running away in fear, he went out to meet his foe.

You can't run from your gaints, you have to face them, if you keep running from them, they will keep taunting you.

And you will not have any peace, they will be out there every morning waiting for you, just like Goliath was there, every morning, (In there face) If your knees are weak because of the giants that keep oppressing you, if you are feeling the urge to run. If you are wanting to go and hide somewhere from it, the word to you this morning is the same one that David spoke to Saul. Let no man's heart fail because of him., (Actually) its your word from the Lord, dont let your heart fail because of it, because the Lord is with you.. He will not leave you are forsake you. The Lord will fight your battle, for you just like He did for David. All of us have to put our trust in Him.

(WORDS THAT BUILDS)

Ephesians. 4:29. K.J.V.

Let no corrupt communication proceed out of your mouth, but that which is good to the use of edifying, that it may ministry grace unto the hearers

Become a source of encouregement to our family, love ones and other's

(1).   Esteem others higher
(2).   Be wise in your speech
(3).   Be encouring
(4).   Be forgiving
(5).   Be understanding
(6).   Zero gossip.
(7).   Share knowledge
(8).   Stay humble
(9).   Be positive
(10.)   Love one another
(11)   Be obedient.
(12)   Be Christ like.

There was a (boy) that ran away from school. He walked around in a (daze) for he did not know the rules

He went to the bus stop, and did not have his fare. Then he said to himself, they just don't care.

He walked a little futher, with no directions to go.

He saw cars, passing him by, at this point he began to cry. So he looked up to the sky, and as he looked down, he saw an old man.

The old man said to him, son, where are you going

The boy said, I don't know the old man said, I am on my way to church, do you want to go,

So, as the old man, took the boy by his hand..

They were walking and talking. The old man began, to tell the boy about Jesus, the one and only man.

When they got to church, the choir were singing

And when they ask, the visitor to stand. The old man told his name, the boy did the same.

There was an old lady humbling a prayer. When she heard the boy, she said out loud, God has answer my prayer.

She said to him, the school has called (me), and said you had ran away. I ask God, to bring you back home, this day. Lets go home, for the table is set.

God of Jehovah, - I am who I am Exodus 3:13-15.

God is Jehovah, M. Kaddath -, The God who sanctifies, Leviticus. 20:7-8

God is Infinite., God is beyond measurement,- Romans. 11:23

God is Omnipotent God is all - powerful, Jeremiah 32:17, 18, 26, 27

God is Good, God is the embodiment of perfect goodness Psalm 119:65-72

God is Love, It embraces each of us personally and intimately - 1-John 4:7:10

God is Jehovah-Jireh, God who provide's Genesis 22:9-14

God is Jehovah-Sholom - The God of peace, Judges 6:16-24

God is Immutable, He is ever perfect and unchanging. Psalm 102-25-28

God is Transcendent, He is existing beyond and above the created universe, Psalm 113, 4-5.

God is Just. We can trust Him to always do whats is right Psalm 75:1-7

God is Holy, His holiness stands apart - unique and incomprehensible Revelation 4:8-11

God is Jehovah-Rophe, Jehovah heals Exodus 15-22-26

God is Self-Sufficient, He can receive nothing that He has not already given us, Acts 17:24-28

God is Omniscient, God is-all-knowing, Psalm 139:1-6

God is Omnipresent, God is everywhere, Psalm 139:7-12

<u>God is Mereciful</u>, Gods mereciful compassion is infinite and inexhaustible, Deuteronomy 4:29-31

<u>God in Sovereign</u>, His sovereignty, He rules His entire creation 1 Chronicles 29:11-13

<u>God is Faithful</u>. God honors His covenant's and fulfills His promises, Psalm 89:1-8

God is above every name, where, every knee, shall bow, and tongue, confess, that He is Lord.

(HOW TO BE GOOD TO OTHERS)

Love the Lord your God with all your heart, with all your soul, with all your strength and with all your mind, and love your neigbor as yourself.

As in (Luke 10:33-34, 35, 36 37)

But a Samaritan, as he was traveling along, came across the man, when the Samaritan saw him, He felt sorry for the man, went to him and cleaned and bandaged his wounds, then he put him on his own animal, brought him to an inn, and took care of him. The next day the Samaritan took out two silver coins and gave them to the innkeeper, he told the innkeeper. Take care of him

If you spend more than, that Ill, pay (you) on my retrurn trip.

The Samitain showed others, how to treat one another, no matter, what, we have to treat, one another, with love, kindness, and compassion.

For it rains on the just and unjust.

God is good

- Wishing you Gods abundant blessing on your birthday. Fill with love and compassion.

    Happy Birthday

- May God continue to pour his love and blessings on you may you recieved, all that you need.

    Happy Birthday

- When flower's are sent on your birthday, means that you will have a beautiful day. Tell everything else to get out of your way, dont forget to get on your knee's and pray.

    Happy Birthday

- May God bless you with health, wealth, happiness strenthen, and love, that you can be hold, for the grace of God, cannot be sold.

    Happy Birthday

- May the Lord bless you and keep you.
  May the Lord smile on you, and protect you. May His love, for ever be with you.

    Happy Birthday

- Birthday birthdays, never go away. The longer you live, the more you learn to pray. Happy Birthday

- You, walk by faith, and not by sight, whatever age you are now, God will make sure that you are, alright.

    Happy Birthday

- Put on your brand new shoe's, you just recieved some good (news)
  What – Its your birthday Happy birthday -, right now.

- Happy Birthday
  May the Lord, keep you may heaven shine upon you may peace follow you and may love sustains you
  Happy Birthday

- Taste and see, that the Lord is good, blessed is the one who takes refuge in him.
  Birthday blessings to you.

- This is another year!
  Another blessing.
  Another day.
  Another second
  Another minite's
  Another hour
  Keep smiling, for this is the day, that the Lord has made
  Happy Birthday.

- Transformation is not five minutes from now, its a present activity. In this moment you can make a diffent choice, and its these small choices and successes, that build up over time to help cultivate a healthy-self-image and self-esteem.

- Knowledge + Understanding = Wisdom, Wisdom + Application = Transformation

- Transformation literally means going, beyond exspection.

- Transformation is about improving, one's self.
  Its about seeking for help
  Its about knocking to fine
  Its about changing your mind.
  Its about leaving, the old things behind

- Transformed people transform people.

- A cattepillor, transform into a butterfly. He crawls he change, then he learns to fly. His colors becomes multiable, his wings strongs he don't stay on the ground for long, for his name has transformed to butterfly.

- Transformation of a persons starts from the inside, if successful, it will show on the outside.

- Embrace each challenge in your life as an opportunity for-self-transformation

- Its not about perfect. Its about effort. And when you bring that effort every single day.
  That's where transformation happen's that's how change, take place.

- To exist is to change to change is to muture to muture is to go on creating oneself endlessly.

- It is our own thoughts that hold the key to miraculous transformation

- If you want to awaken all of humanity then awaken all of yourself. If you want to eliminate the suffering in the world, then eliminate all that is dark and nagative in your self. Truly, the greatest gift you have to give is that of your own-self-transformation.

I would like to take this time to give God, all the glory, for allowing me to complete this book.

When God, says yes things comes forth.

To whom, reads the book, I pray, that some of the words encourage your heart. Always look up and give God, the praise

I would like to take this time, to thank <u>Sarah Sanders</u>, for pushing me, and encouring me to finish the (book). I have learn, that whatever, that a person put their mind to it will come to pass. We have to have a made up mind. A determine heart. A will to do so.

Whatever God, has for a person, it is only for that person. This book was placed is my heart some years ago. But, as we all do, I put the book down, and would pick it up on occasion.

Life is the only thing we have, we have to make the best of each day. My prayer is that this book get in the hand of person's, that needs it most.

No matter what position one holds, we all need encouragement.

Take time each day to tell someone how much you love them.

In closing, once again

For God, so loved the world, that he gave his only begotten son, that whosoever believeth in him should not perish, but have everlasting life
John 3:16

The one and only book
<u>Differt Varitys, title</u>

Auther. Bettie Roberson!

(Peace)

Printed in the United States
By Bookmasters